LOUNGE DESIGN

daab

Architects / Designers	Location	Page

With the term lounge, one associates a place accompanied with lingering physical relaxation and a pleasant atmosphere. Nowadays, lounges are ever more prevalent because it is exactly the companies – primarily the airlines and hotels – that long ago realized they need to offer their customers and guests more than just the usual services. On top of that, other companies, public facilities, and industry are increasingly creating space in their showrooms and exhibition booths that offer a relaxing atmosphere and for a while let one forget the stress of the daily grind. Relaxing in contemporarily designed surroundings thus becomes an attitude toward life. The volume at hand shows over 60 international design examples that illuminate exactly this lounge feeling from various perspectives and so offers an up-to-date and comprehensive survey of this topic for the first time. Divided into chapters on airline lounges, corporate lounges, public facilities, gastronomy, hotels, and trade fair and events, contractors, planners, and interested parties will find a wealth of inspiring and useful stimuli.

Mit dem Begriff Lounge assoziiert man einen Ort, der mit körperlicher Entspannung und einer angenehmen Stimmung von Verweilen einhergeht. Lounges sind uns heutzutage immer gegenwärtiger, weil gerade Unternehmen – allen voran Airlines und Hotels – längst erkannt haben, dass sie für ihre Kunden und Gäste mehr bieten müssen als die übliche Dienstleistung. Aber auch viele andere Unternehmen, öffentliche Einrichtungen und die Industrie schaffen zunehmend in ihren Showrooms oder auf Messeständen Räume, die eine Atmosphäre der Erholung bieten und den Stress des Alltages für eine Weile vergessen lassen. Relaxen in einer zeitgemäß designten Umgebung wird so zu einem Lebensgefühl. Der vorliegende Band zeigt über 60 internationale Planungsbeispiele, die eben dieses Gefühl Lounge aus den unterschiedlichsten Perspektiven beleuchtet und damit erstmals einen aktuellen und umfassenden Überblick über dieses Thema gibt. Eingeteilt in die Kapitel Airline Lounges, Unternehmens-Lounges, öffentliche Einrichtungen, Gastronomie, Hotels, sowie Messen- und Events finden Auftraggeber, Planer und Interessierte eine Fülle inspirierender und nützlicher Anregungen.

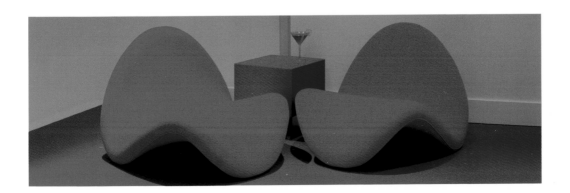

Nous associons au concept de Lounge un lieu permettant la détente physique ainsi qu'une agréable ambiance de repos. Les Lounges sont aujourd'hui de plus en plus présents dans notre environnement, parce que justement les entreprises – et notamment les lignes aériennes et les hôtels – ont compris depuis longtemps qu'ils doivent offrir à leurs clients et invités plus que le service habituel. Mais de nombreuses autres entreprises, organismes publics ainsi que l'industrie aménagent aussi de plus en plus de showrooms ou de locaux sur un stand de foire, ceux-ci offrant une atmosphère de repos ou faisant oublier un moment le stress de la vie quotidienne. Se relaxer dans un cadre de design contemporain devient ainsi un art de vivre. Le présent volume montre plus de 60 exemples de planification internationaux, et éclaire justement cette sensation de Lounge sous les perspectives les plus diverses, donnant ainsi pour la première fois une vue d'ensemble actuelle et étendue sur ce sujet. La répartition dans les chapitres Lounges de lignes aériennes, Lounges d'entreprises, bâtiments publics, gastronomie, hôtels, et foires et manifestations permet aux clients, planificateurs et personnes intéressées de trouver une multitude de propositions utiles et pleines d'inspiration.

Con el término „lounge" uno asocia un lugar en el que se disfruta de un ambiente agradable que invita a una placentera estancia y al relajamiento corporal. Los lounges son cada vez más populares, ya que precisamente las empresas - y ante todo las compañías aéreas y los hoteles – hace tiempo que han reconocido la necesidad de ofrecer a sus clientes y huéspedes algo más que los servicios usuales. Pero también muchas otras empresas, entidades estatales y la industria crean cada vez más espacios en sus showrooms y stands de feria, en los que se respira un ambiente de relax, donde uno puede olvidar por un momento el estrés cotidiano. Así, relajarse en un entorno decorado al estilo contemporáneo se convierte en un estilo de vida. El presente tomo muestra más de 60 ejemplos de proyectos internacionales que iluminan este estilo de vida representado por los lounges desde las más diversas perspectivas, ofreciendo con ello el primer compendio actual y completo sobre este tema. En este tomo, que está dividido en los capítulos Lounges de aeropuertos, empresas, entidades públicas, gastronomía, hoteles, ferias y acontecimientos, los clientes, planificadores e interesados encontrarán multitud de útiles e inspiradoras ideas.

Si associa al termine della Lounge un luogo che abbina il relax ad una gradevole atmosfera per la sosta. Al giorno d'oggi, abbiamo sempre più presenti le lounges, proprio perché le imprese – innanzitutto le compagnie aeree e gli alberghi – hanno da tempo riconosciuto che devono offrire più che gli abituali servizi ai loro clienti ed ospiti. Ma anche molte altre imprese, enti pubblici e l'industria all'interno delle loro showrooms e stands fieristici creano sempre più spesso ambienti che offrono un'atmosfera rilassante, lasciando che lo stress della vita quotidiana per un momento svanisca. Concedersi il relax in un ambiente dal design contemporaneo, diventa così uno stile di vita. Il presente volume dimostra oltre 60 esempi di progettazione internazionali che dalle più svariate prospettive illuminano per l'appunto questa sensazione Lunge, fornendo per la prima volta un'attuale e vasta panoramica su questo tema. Con la sua suddivisione nei capitoli: Lounges di compagnie aeree, d'imprese, di enti pubblici, della gastronomia, di alberghi, nonché di fiere e relativi eventi, i committenti, i progettisti e gli interessati trovano un'abbondanza di suggerimenti ispiranti ed utili.

COMPANIES

DELUGAN_MEISSL ARCHITEKTURBÜRO ZT-GESELLSCHAFT I VIENNA
Sandoz Novartis
Office Lounge
Vienna, Austria I 2003
Photos: Rupert Steiner I Vienna

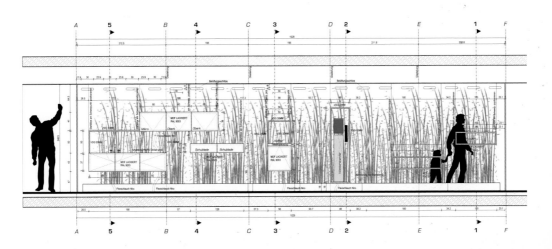

DESIGN COMPANY AGENTUR GMBH I MUNICH
AOL
Promotion Lounge
OMD Düsseldorf, Germany I 2002, 2003
Photos: Michael Igenweyen I Munich

GREGO & SMOLENICKY ARCHITEKTUR GMBH I ZURICH
Accenture
New Office Campus Kronberg
Kronberg, Germany I 2002
Photos: Walter Mair I Zurich

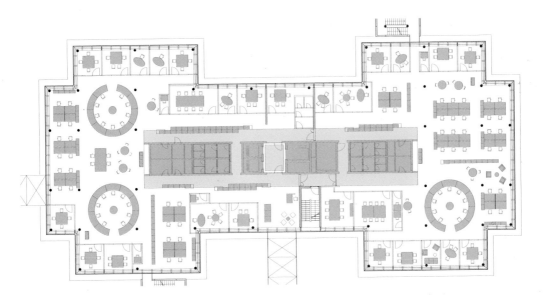

HPP HENTRICH-PETSCHNIGG & PARTNER KG | COLOGNE
Furnishing by Walter Knoll
Allianz AG
Lobby
Frankfurt/Main, Germany | 2001
Photos: H. G. Esch | Hennef/Sieg

ILYA CORPORATION | TOKYO
TMI Associates
Office Lounge
Tokyo, Japan | 2003
Photos: Nacása & Partners Inc. | Tokyo

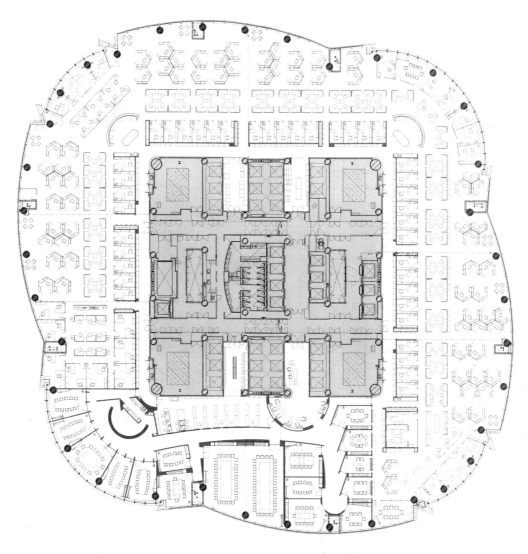

KPMB KUWABARA PAYNE MCKENNA BLUMBERG ARCHITECTS | TORONTO
Roy Thomson Hall
Lexus Lounge
Toronto, Canada | 2004
Photos: Peter Sellar | Toronto

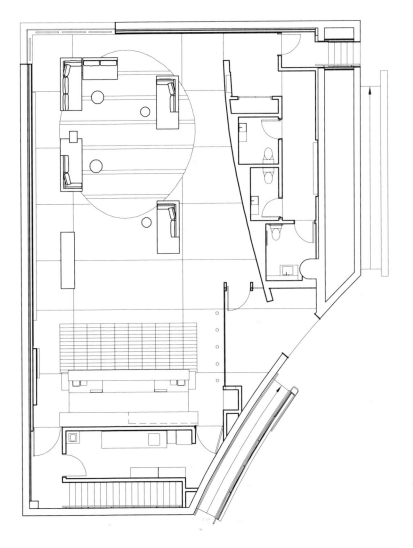

MIKULANDRA-MACKAT ARCHITEKTIN, KOSCHE DESIGN | BERLIN

Fritzsch & Mackat Werbeagentur
Office Lounge
Berlin, Germany | 2002
Photos: Werner Huthmacher | Berlin

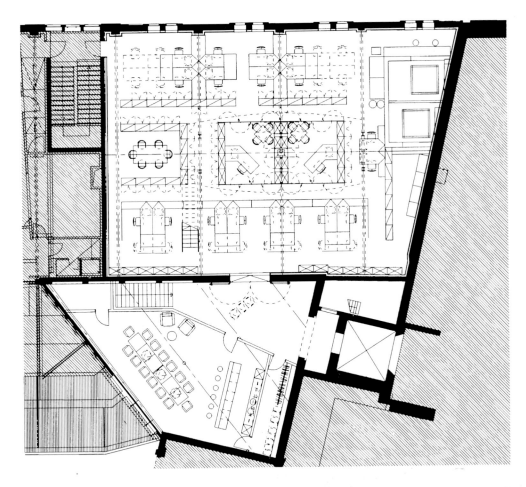

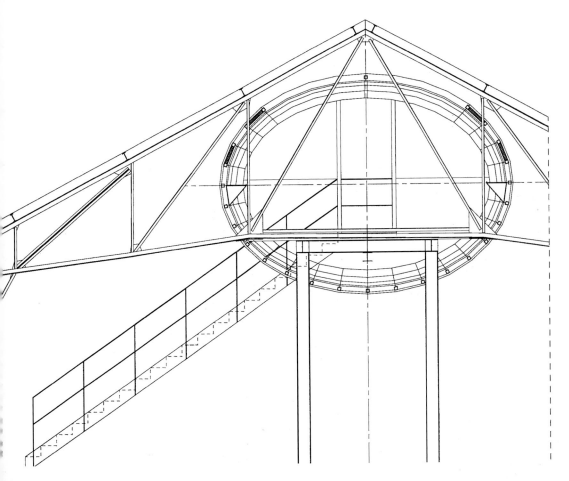

NETHERBLU | DÜSSELDORF
Sparkasse
Lobby
Bremen, Germany | 2003
Photos: Joerg Hempel | Aachen

RLD RAISER LOPES DESIGNERS | STUTTGART
BOSS Outlet
Espresso Lounge
Metzingen, Germany | 2004
Photos: Courtesy RLD RaiserLopesDesigners | Stuttgart

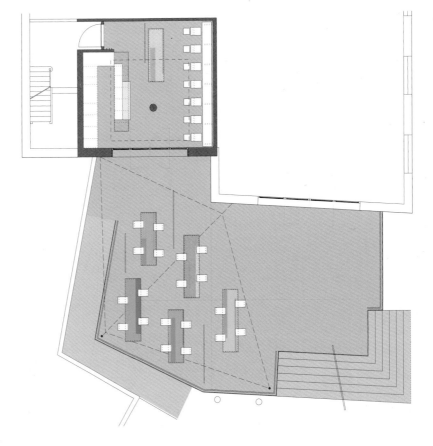

SEHW ARCHITEKTEN | HAMBURG, BERLIN
Universal Music Group
Lobby
Berlin, Germany | 2002
Photos: Jürgen Schmidt | Cologne

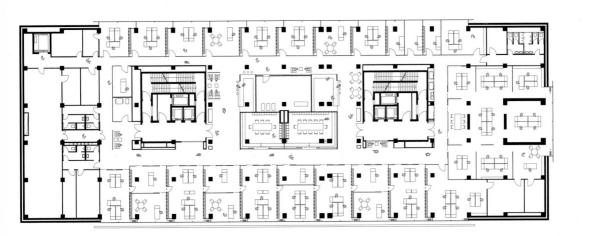

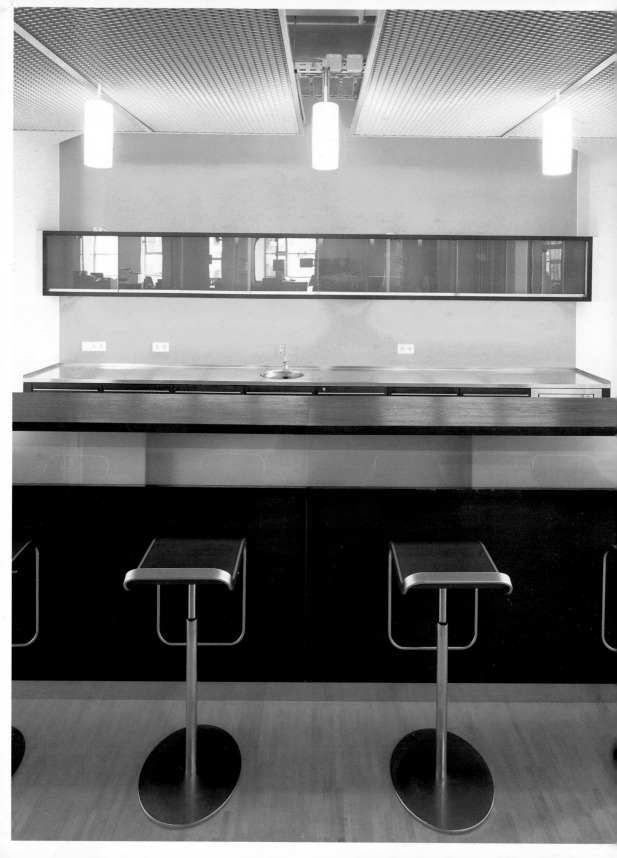

STUDIO POWER | MILAN WITH E. CARLSON
Celux
Top floor of Louis Vuitton Building Omotesando
Tokyo, Japan | 2002
Photos: Daici Ano | Tokyo

CULTURE, ENTERTAINMENT, PUBLIC

3DELUXE | WIESBADEN
Cyberhelvetia Credit Suisse Group
Expo.02
Arteplage Biel, Switzerland | 2002
Photos: Emanuel Raab | Wiesbaden

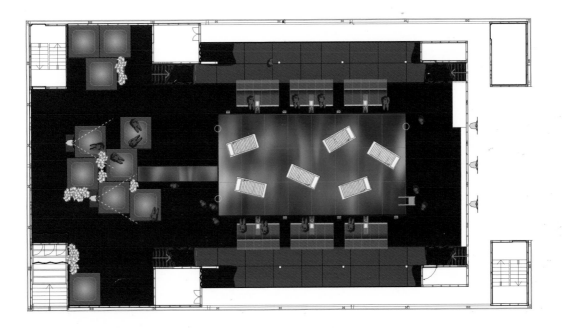

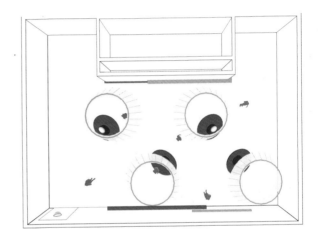

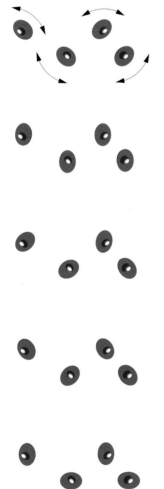

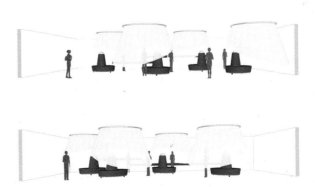

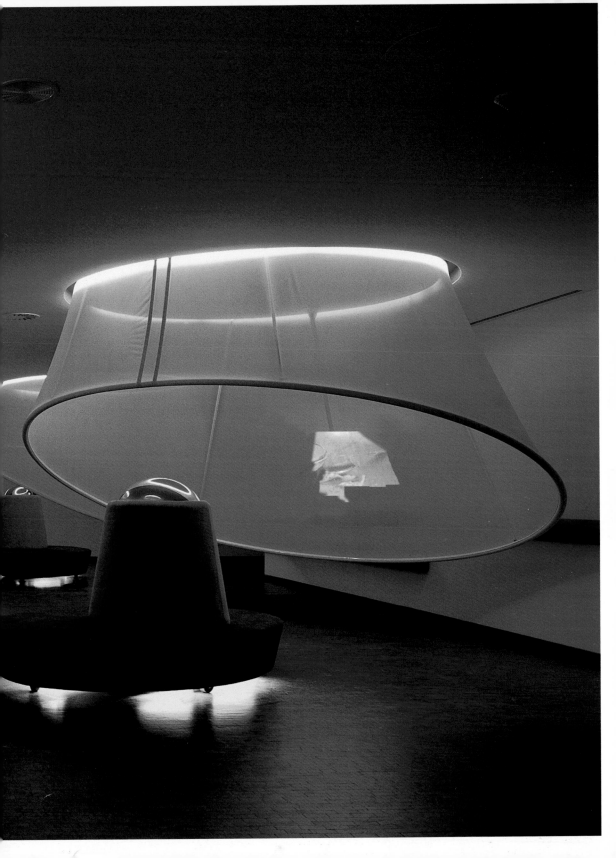

AG4 MEDIATECTURE COMPANY | **COLOGNE**
DB Deutsche Bahn
Lounge Expo 2002
Hannover, Germany | 2002
Photos: Uwe Spoering | Cologne

ATELIER BRÜCKNER | STUTTGART
Haus der Geschichte Baden-Württemberg
Baden-Württemberg Lounge
Stuttgart, Germany | 2002
Photos: Bernd Eidenmüller | Stuttgart

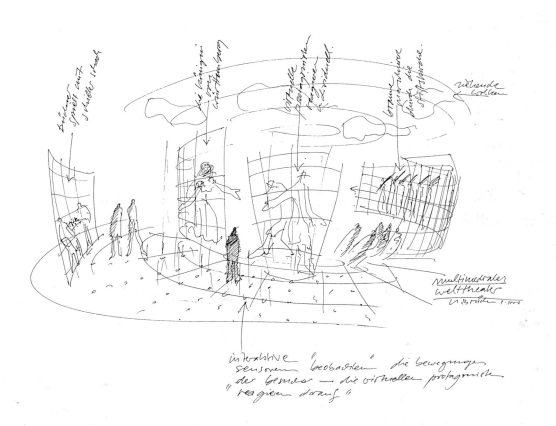

BURKHALTER SUMI ARCHITEKTEN GMBH | ZURICH
Pavillon Onoma
Expo.02
Arteplage Yvérdon-les-Bains, Switzerland | 2002
Photos: Heinrich Helfenstein | Zurich

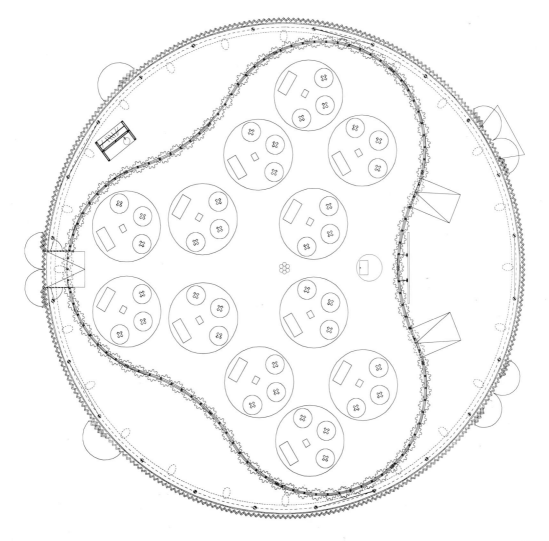

FOSTER AND PARTNERS | LONDON
Furnishing by Walter Knoll
Reichstag Building
Lobby Lounge, Restaurant & Bar
Berlin, Germany | 1999
Photos: H. G. Esch | Hennef/Sieg

FRANKEN ARCHITEKTEN | FRANKFURT/MAIN
BMW & Deutsches Museum The Bubble
Munich, Germany | 2000
Photos: Fritz Busam | Berlin

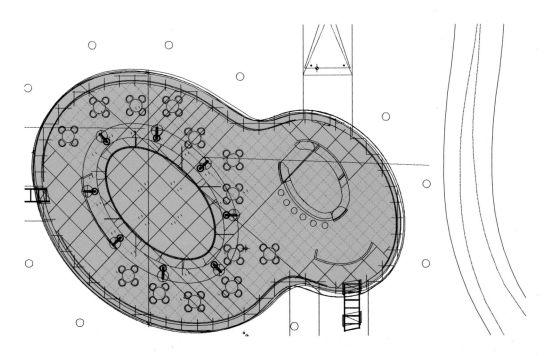

GRAMAZIO & KOHLER | ZURICH
sWISH* Pavillon
Vip Lounge, IBM Schweiz, Swiss Re
Expo.02
Arteplage Biel, Switzerland | 2002
Photos: Atelier Roman Keller | Zurich

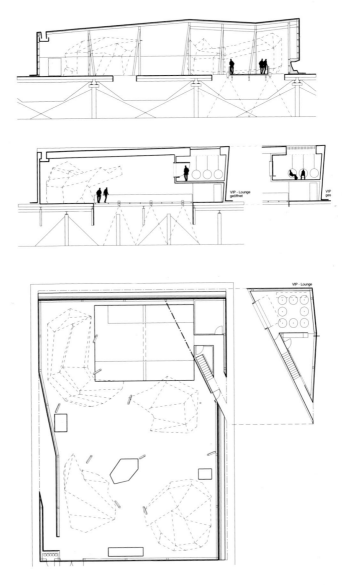

J. MAYER H. ARCHITEKTEN | BERLIN
Stylepark
XXI. Weltkongress der Architekten
Berlin, Germany | 2002
Photos: Uwe Walter | Berlin

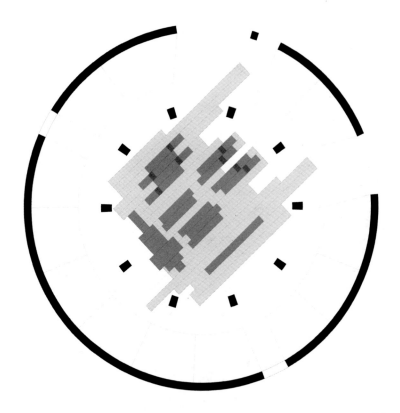

SÖHNE & PARTNER | VIENNA
Babenberger Passage
Club & Event Location
Vienna, Austria | 2003
Photos: Alexander Koller | Vienna

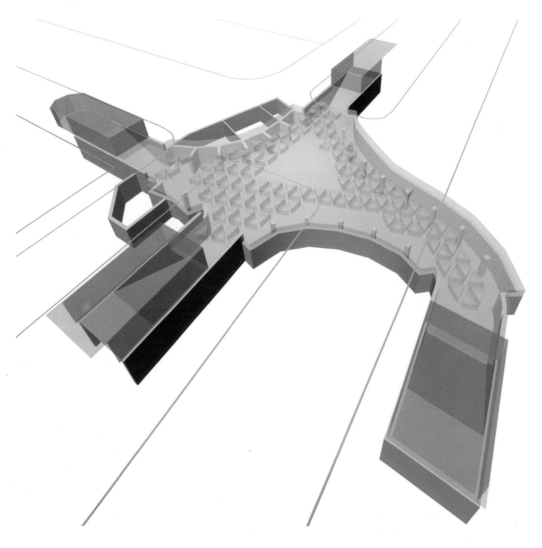

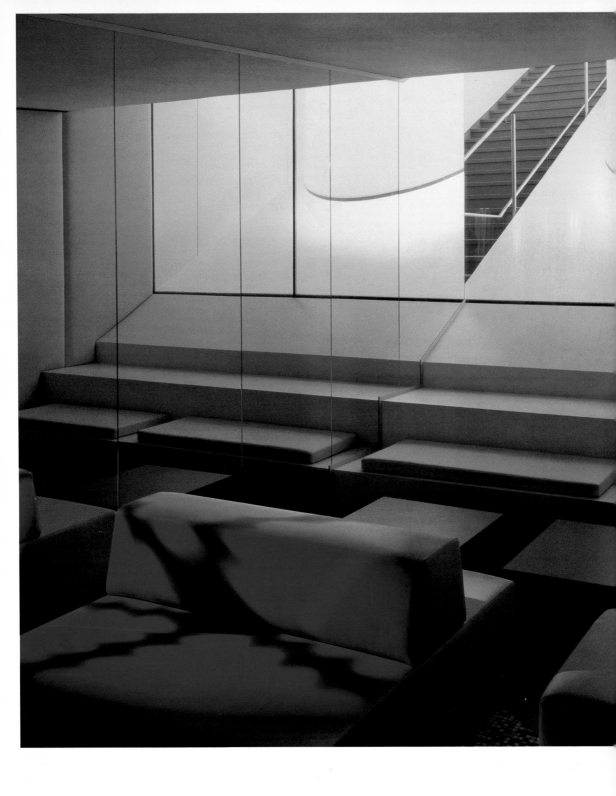

GASTRONOMY

BERND BEISSE | NUREMBERG
Club Wega
Club & Restaurant
Nuremberg, Germany | 2003
Photos: Courtesy Club Wega | Nuremberg

BOTTEGA + EHRHARDT ARCHITEKTEN | STUTTGART
Suite 212
Club, Bar & Lounge
Stuttgart, Germany | 2001
Photos: Alexander Fischer | Stuttgart

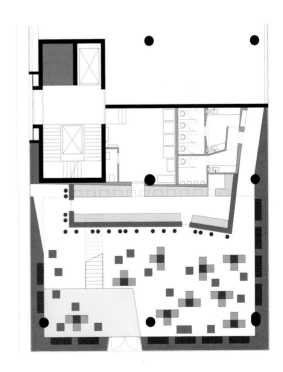

STEPHANE DUPOUX | MIAMI
Pearl
Club & Restaurant
Miami, USA | 2003
Photos: Courtesy Pearl | Miami

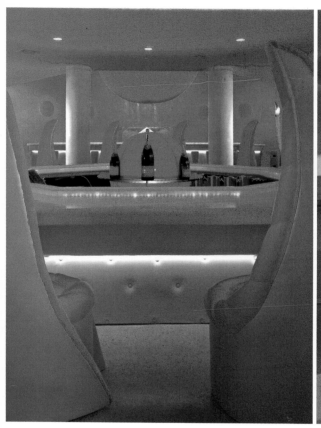

GREGO & SMOLENICKY ARCHITEKTUR GMBH I ZURICH
Bar Sport 024
Zurich, Switzerland I 2002
Photos: Walter Mair I Zurich

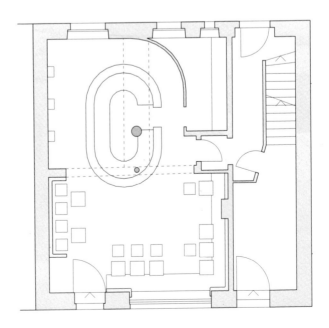

JULIA HÖLZEL, PATRICK FERRIER | MUNICH
Nektar
Club, Bar & Restaurant
Munich, Germany | 2003
Photos: Derek Henthorn | Munich

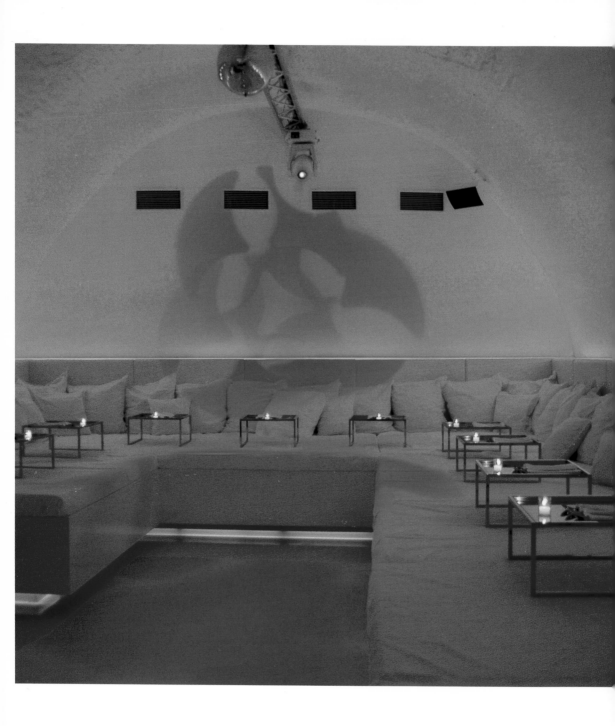

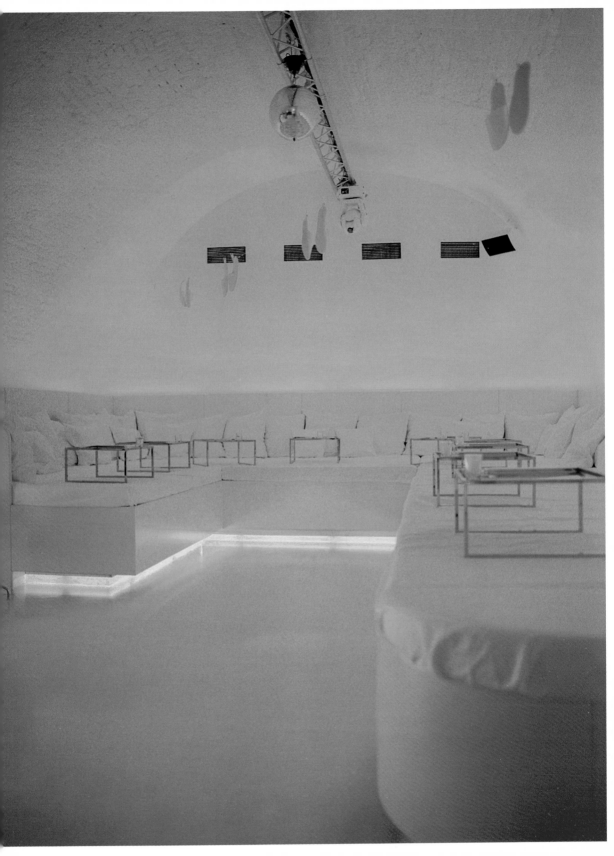

SCOTT KESTER INC. | **NEW YORK**
Kemia
Club & Restaurant
New York, USA | 2003
Photos: Scott Kester | New York

ORA-ITO | PARIS
Furnishing by De Sede
Le Cabaret Paris
Club & Restaurant
Paris, France | 2003
Photos: Matteo Manduzio | Munich

ORBIT DESIGN STUDIO | BANGKOK
Bed Supperclub Bangkok
Club, Bar & Lounge
Bangkok, Thailand | 2000
Photos: Courtesy Bed Supperclub | Bangkok

PLAJER & FRANZ STUDIO | BERLIN
Universum Lounge
Restaurant, Bar & Lounge
Berlin, Germany | 2000
Photos: Karl Bongartz | Berlin

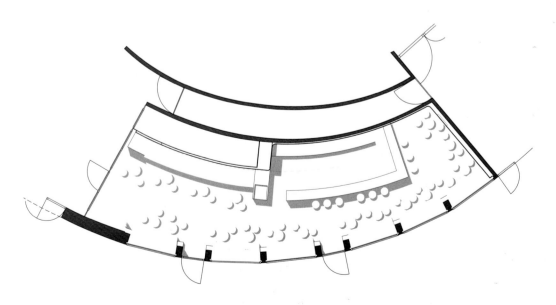

YASUI HIDEO ATELIER | TOKYO
Club Now
Restaurant & Lounge
Tokyo, Japan | 2001
Photos: Nacasa & Partners Inc. | Tokyo

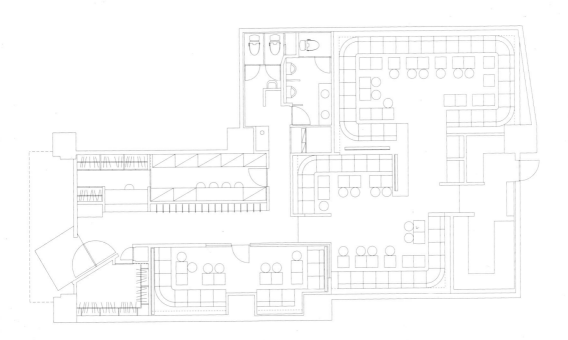

HOTELS

3META | AUGSBURG, MUNICH
25hours Hotel
Lobby & Lounge
Hamburg, Germany | 2003
Photos: Martin Kunz | Stuttgart

GUIDO CIOMPI | FLORENCE
The Gray
Lobby & Lounge
Milan, Italy | 2003
Photos: Martin Kunz, Roland Bauer | Stuttgart

GRAFT ARCHITEKTEN | **BERLIN, LOS ANGELES**
Q! Hotel
Lobby & Lounge
Berlin, Germany | 2004
Photos: Fotostudio Dirk Schaper | Berlin

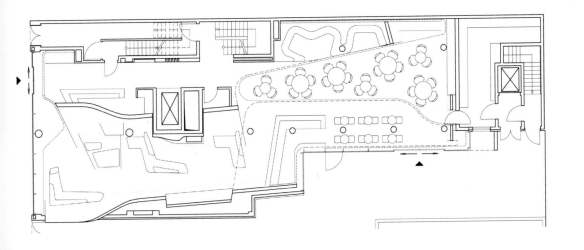

KING & ROSELLI ARCHITETTI | ROME
Es Hotel
Restaurant & Bar
Rome, Italy | 2003
Photos: Santi Calca, Luigi Filatici, Jose King

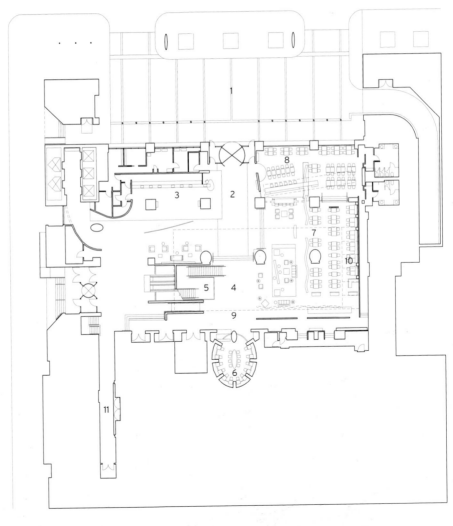

MATALI CRASSET | PARIS
Hi Hotel
Lobby & Lounge
Nice, France | 2003
Photos: Uwe Spoering | Cologne

RUY OHTAKE | SAO PAULO
Hotel Unique
Lobby, Bar & Café
Sao Paulo, Brazil | 2003
Photos: Courtesy Hotel Unique | Sao Paulo

SCHUSTER, PECHTOLD & PARTNERS | DUBAI
Al Maha
Lobby & Lounge
Dubai, UAE | 1999
Photos: Martin Kunz | Stuttgart

STUDIO GAIA | **NEW YORK**
W Hotel Mexico City
Lobby & Lounge
Mexico City, Mexico | 2002
Photos: Ilan Waisbrod | New York

ADAM D.TIHANY | NEW YORK
The Aleph
Lounge & Bar
Rome, Italy | 2003
Photos: Courtesy Aleph | Rome

YABU PUSHELBERG | TORONTO
W Hotel Times Square N.Y.
Lobby, Bar & Lounge
New York, USA | 2001
Photos: Evan Dion | Toronto

SPORTS, HEATLHCLUBS, EVENTS & FAIRS

3DELUXE | WIESBADEN
Football Globe
Promotion Lounge
Berlin, Germany | 2003
Photos: Emanuel Raab | Wiesbaden, Wolfgang Stahl | Berlin

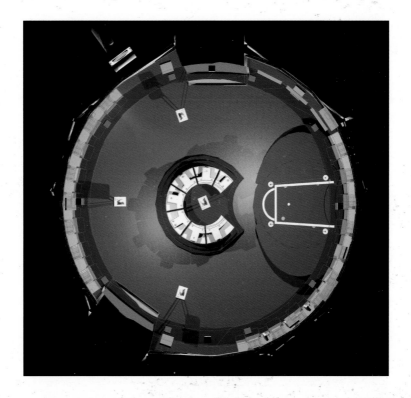

BOUROULLEC | SAINT-DENIS
Ideal House Special Bouroullec
IMM Cologne
Cologne, Germany | 2004
Photos: Courtesy IMM Cologne

CHRISTIAN WERNER INDUSTRIAL DESIGN | **HOLLENSTEDT/APPEL**
Rolf Benz Cafélounge
IMM Cologne 2004
Cologne, Germany | 2004
Photos: H. G. Esch | Hennef/Sieg

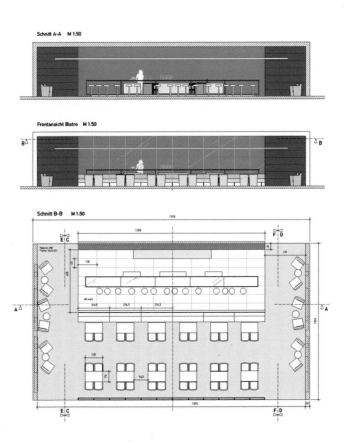

DESIGN COMPANY AGENTUR GMBH | MUNICH
Sony Ericsson
CeBIT Communication Lounge
Hannover, Germany | 2004
Photos: Michael Igenweyen | Munich

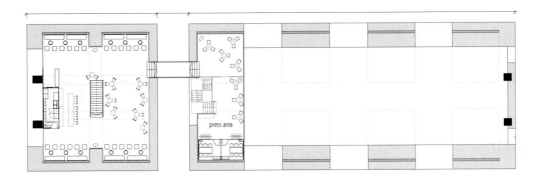

Home Server

DESIGN COMPANY AGENTUR GMBH | **MUNICH**
Sony
CeBIT Connectivity Lounge
Hannover, Germany | 2003
Photos: Michael Igenweyen | Munich

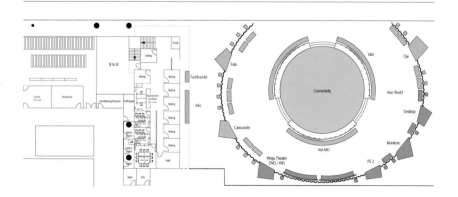

MAHMOUDIEHDESIGN | BERLIN, LONDON
L'Oréal VIP Club
Berlinale Berlin
Berlin, Germany | 2003
Photos: Zumtobel Staff / Fritz Busam | Berlin

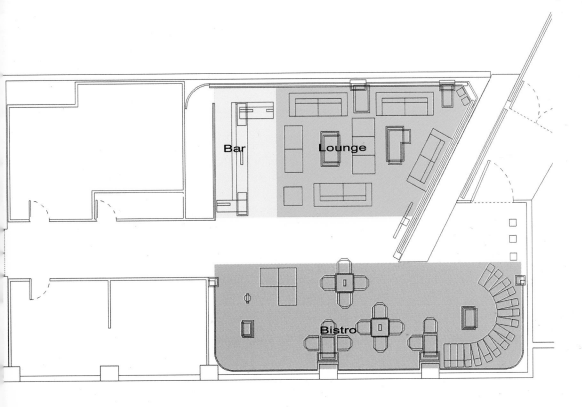

BMW Concept M5

**Où nous mènera notre
succès en compétition?
Directement sur la route.**

Avec la M5, BMW Motorsport a un héritage de haute performance. Le mariage entre performances dignes de la compétition automobile et caractéristiques d'une berline de prestige génère un plaisir de conduire sans compromis. Au plus haut niveau technologique.

**Wohin unser Erfolg auf
der Rennstrecke führt?
Direkt auf die Straße.**

Seit 20 Jahren steht BMW M wie kein anderes Serienfahrzeug für höchsten Anspruch auf der Straße. Die Verbindung von rennsporterprobter Leistungsfähigkeit mit Eigenschaften einer Luxuslimousine sorgt für kompromisslosen Fahrspaß auf technisch höchstem Niveau.

PLAJER & FRANZ STUDIO | BERLIN
BMW Messelounge
Automobilsalon Geneva
Geneva, Switzerland | 2004
Photos: diephotodesigner.de | Berlin

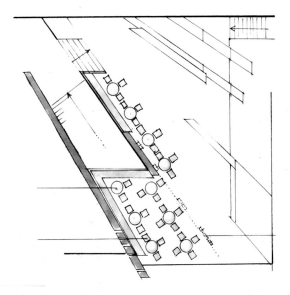

PLAJER & FRANZ STUDIO I **BERLIN**
BMW Messelounge
IAA Internationale Automobilausstellung Frankfurt
Frankfurt, Germany I 2003
Photos: Fritz Busam, Alexander Plajer I Berlin

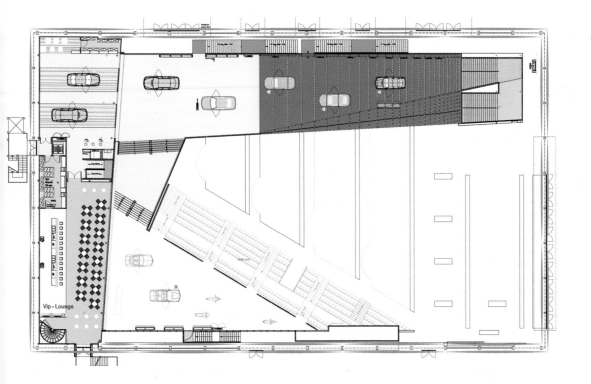

SEHW ARCHITEKTEN | **HAMBURG, BERLIN**
Holmes Place Lifestyle Club
Salzburg, Austria | 2003
Photos: Jürgen Schmidt | Cologne

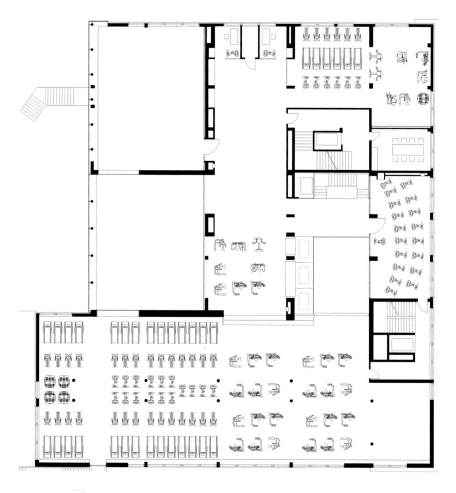

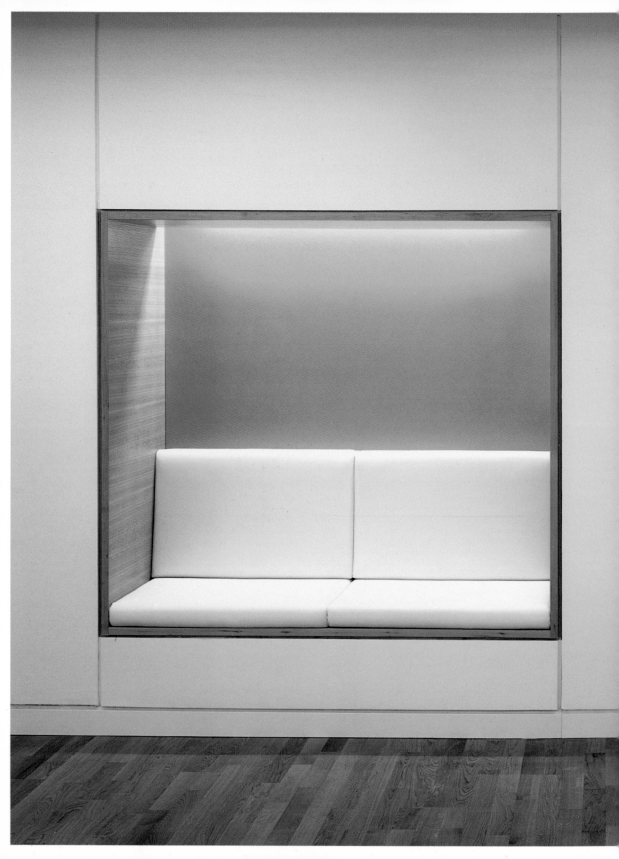

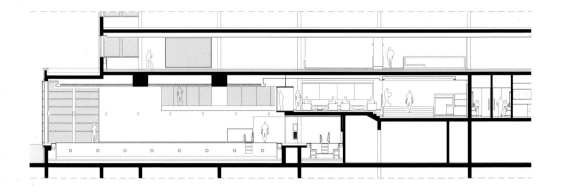

SEHW ARCHITEKTEN | HAMBURG, BERLIN
Holmes Place Lifestyle Club
Hamburg, Germany | 2003
Photos: Jürgen Schmidt | Cologne

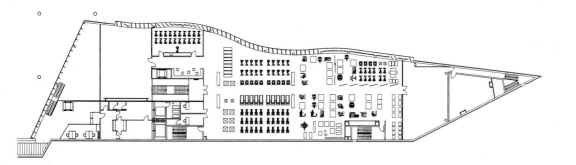

TRAFFIC

BREWER DAVIDSON & CUNNINGHAM MARTYN DESIGN | AUCKLAND
Koru Club Lounge, Air New Zealand
Auckland Airport
Auckland, New Zealand | 2002
Photos: Kevin Brewer | Auckland

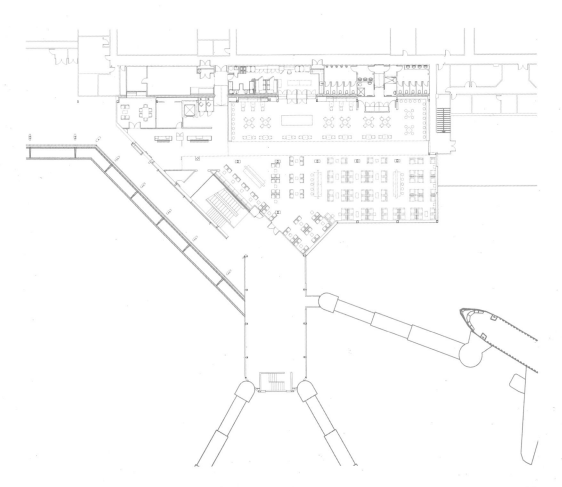

**JONATHAN CLARKE OF ECHO SOUNDER ǀ LONDON
WITH ILYA CORPORATION ǀ TOKYO**
Virgin Atlantic Airways
Narita International Airport
Chiba, Japan ǀ 1999
Photos: Yoshiteru Baba ǀ Tokyo

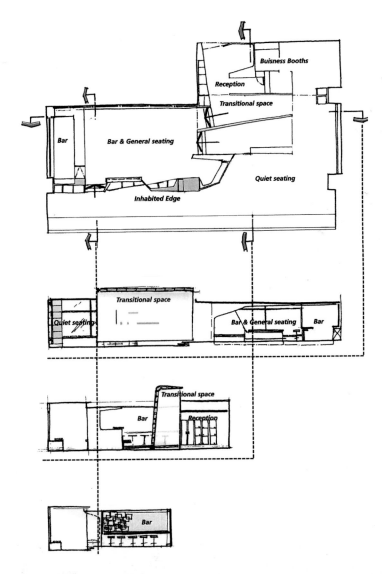

321

EIGHT INC. | **SAN FRANCISCO**
Virgin Atlantic Airways Clubhouse SFO
San Francisco International Airport
San Francisco, USA | 2001
Photos: Timothy Hursley | Little Rock

ERIC GIZARD | **PARIS**
Air France First and Business Class Lounges CDG 2E
Airport CDG Paris
Paris, France | 2003
Photos: Luc Boegly | Paris

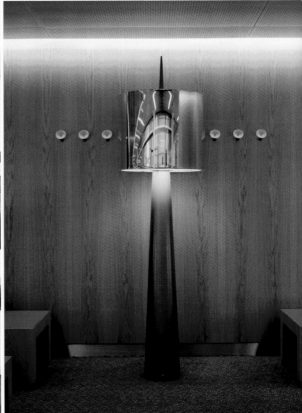

HOLLIN RADOSKE ARCHITEKTEN | FRANKFURT
Lufthansa Senator Lounge MUC
Munich Airport
Munich, Germany | 2003
Photos: Johann Hinrichs | Munich

JOHN PAWSON | **LONDON**
Cathay Pacific The Wing
Hongkong Chek Lap Kok Airport
Hong Kong, China | 1988
Photos: Nacása & Partners Inc. | Tokyo

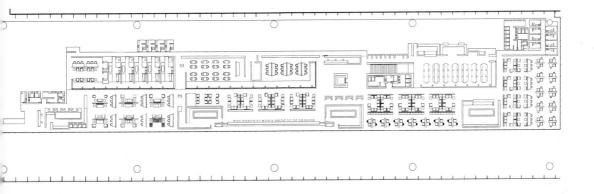

KPMB KUWABARA PAYNE MCKENNA BLUMBERG ARCHITECTS | TORONTO
WITH LIZ ETZOLD ARCHITEKTIN | ZURICH
Star Alliance Lounge Zurich
Zurich International Airport
Zurich, Switzerland | 2001
Photos: Ted Fahn, Walter Mair | Toronto

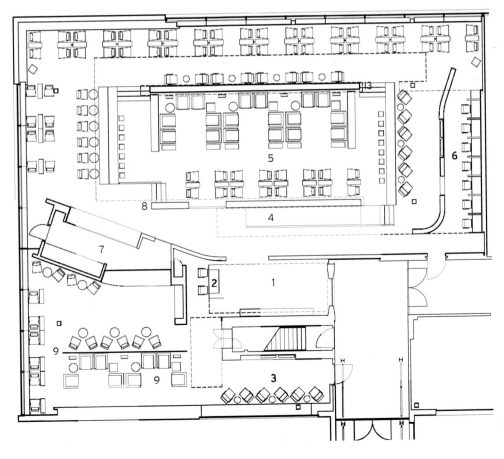

KPMB KUWABARA PAYNE MCKENNA BLUMBERG ARCHITECTS | TORONTO

Air Canada Maple Leaf Lounge
Toronto International Airport
Toronto, Canada | 2004
Photos: David Whittaker | Toronto

AUSTRIAN AIRLINES WITH LANDOR ASSOCIATES | HAMBURG
Austrian Airlines Business Lounge
Vienna Schwechat International Airport
Vienna, Austria | 2003
Photos: Carlos de Mello, Lukas Beck | Vienna,
Landor Associates | Hamburg

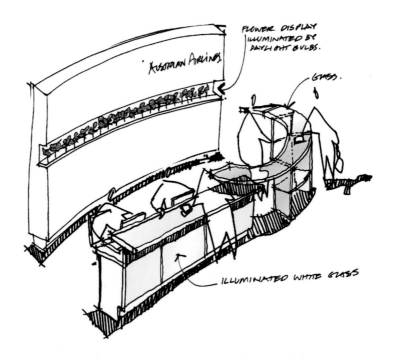

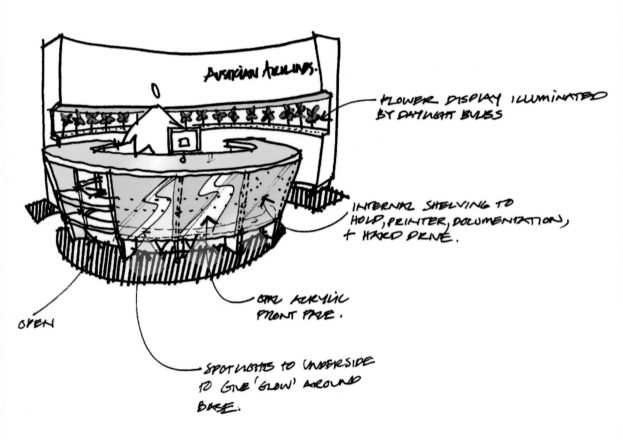

AVSTRIAN AIRLINES.

FLOWER DISPLAY ILLUMINATED
BY DAYLIGHT BULBS

INTERNAL SHELVING TO
HOLD, PRINTER, DOCUMENTATION,
+ HARD DRIVE.

OPAL ACRYLIC
FRONT FACE.

OVEN

SPOT LIGHTS TO UNDERSIDE
TO GIVE 'GLOW' AROUND
BASE.

ILKKA SUPPANEN | HELSINKI
Furnishing by Artek
Artek Lounge
Helsinki-Vantaa Airport
Helsinki, Finland | 2003
Photos: Courtesy Artek | Helsinki

WINKREATIVE I ZURICH
WITH MACH ARCHITEKTUR I ZURICH
Swiss First Study
Nightliner Study
Projects
Renderings: Courtesy Mach Architektur I Zurich

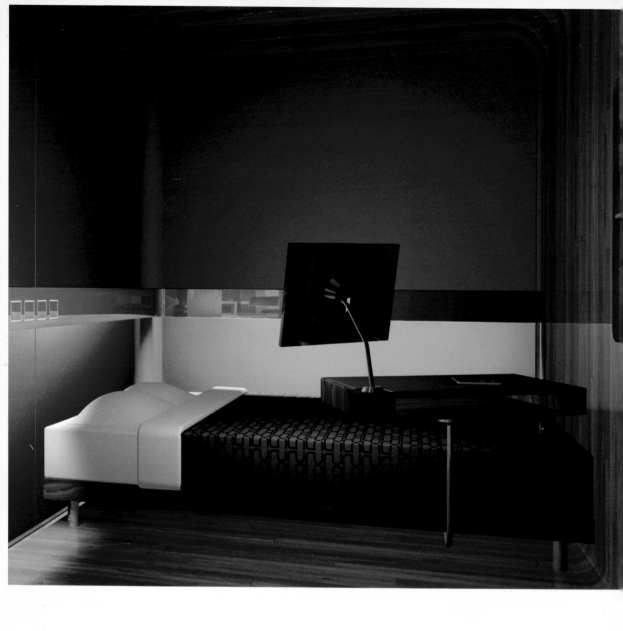

INDEX

copyright © 2004 daab gmbh

published and distributed worldwide by
daab gmbh
stadtwaldgürtel 57
d - 50935 cologne | germany

t +49-221-94 10 74 0
f +49-221-94 10 74 1

mail@daab-online.de
www.daab-online.de

publisher ralf daab
rdaab@daab-online.de

art director feyyaz
mail@feyyaz.com

produced by fusion publishing gmbh, stuttgart | germany
www.fusion-publishing.com

editorial direction by martin nicholas kunz

edited by joachim fischer (brandaffairs stuttgart),
patricia massó (fusion publishing)

introduction by professor axel müller-schöll,
chair for interior design of the department of design.
university of art and design, burg giebichenstein,
halle (saale), germany

prepress and imaging: thomas hausberg, florian höch

translations
english: robert kaplan
french: ludovic allain
spanish: margarita celdràn-kuhl
italian: jacqueline rizzo

printed in spain

isbn 3-937718-01-X

D.L.: B-26749-04